A Dog's Life

First published by Parragon in 2010

Parragon
Queen Street House
4 Queen Street
Bath BA1 1HE, UK

ISBN: 978-1-4075-8641-0

Printed in China

A Dog's Life

inspiration for dog lovers everywhere

Bath New York Singapore Hong Kong Cologne Delhi Melbourne

A dog is man's best friend.

Dogs are
miracles

with paws.

Susan Ariel Rainbow Kennedy (Attrib), Author

A good dog deserves a good bone. American proverb

The reason a dog has **so many friends** is that he wags his tail instead of his tongue.

Unknown

There is
no psychiatrist in the world
like a
puppy

licking your face. Bern Williams, Author

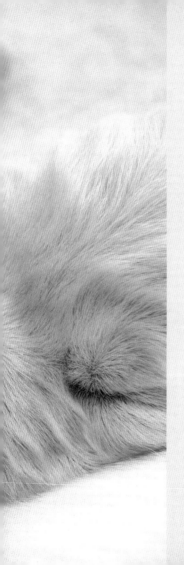

The
biggest
dog

has been a

pup.

Joaquin Miller

A dog

is one of the remaining

reasons

why some people can be persuaded

to go for a walk.

OA Battista, Author

My little dog -

a heartbeat

at my feet.

Edith Wharton, Novelist

Dogs are not our whole life,

but they make ◄

lives whole.

Roger Caras, Wildlife photographer

If your dog doesn't

like someone

you

probably

shouldn't

either. Unknown

To **live** long,

eat like a **cat,**

drink

like a dog.

German proverb

Dogs feel very **strongly** that they should always go with you in the car, in case the need should arise for them to **bark** nothing right in your ear.

Dave Barry, Columnist

A door

is what a dog is

perpetually on the

wrong side of.

Ogden Nash, Poet

If you can look
at a dog and not feel

vicarious
excitement

and affection,

you must be a cat.

Unknown

Anybody
who doesn't know what soap
tastes like
has never
washed a dog.

Franklin P Jones, Businessman

The dog was created specially for children.

He is the god of frolic.

Henry Ward Beecher, Clergyman

35

Yesterday I was a dog.

Today I'm a dog.

Tomorrow I'll probably

still be a dog.

Sigh!

There's so little hope for

advancement.

Charles M Schulz, Cartoonist

Don't accept

your dog's admiration
as conclusive evidence
that you are wonderful.

Ann Landers, Columnist

My goal in life is to be as good as my dog already thinks I am.

Unknown

a person

No matter how little money

having a dog makes

and how few possessions you own,

you rich. Louis Sabin, Author

The cat will mew and the dog will have his day.

William Shakespeare, Poet and playwright

It is nought good a sleeping hound wake.

Geoffrey Chaucer, Author and poet

Dogs are better
than human beings
because they know
but do not tell.

A puppy is but a dog,

plus

high spirits,

and

minus

common sense.

Agnes Repplier, Essayist

Every dog is a lion at home.

HG Bohn, Publisher

Dachshund:
a half-a-dog high
and a
dog-and-a-half long.

Henry Louis Mencken, Journalist

The difference between cats and dogs is,

dogs come

when they are called,

cats take a message

and get back to you.

Unknown

Man is a dog's **idea** of what **God** should be.

Holbrook Jackson, Journalist

There is no faith which has never been broken, except that of a truly

faithful dog.

Konrad Lorenz, Zoologist

One reason

a dog can be such a comfort

when you're feeling blue

is that he doesn't try

to find out why.

Unknown

Properly trained, a man can be a dog's best friend.

Corey Ford, Humorist and author

When a dog wants to hang out the "Do Not Disturb" sign, as all of us do now and then, he is regarded as a **traitor** to his species.

Ramona C Albert

The most
affectionate
creature
in the world

is a wet dog.

Ambrose Bierce, Journalist

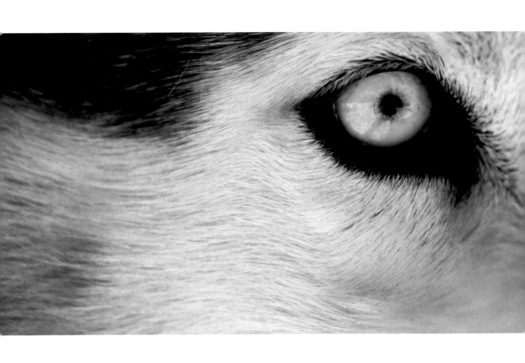

Life is like a dog sled team.

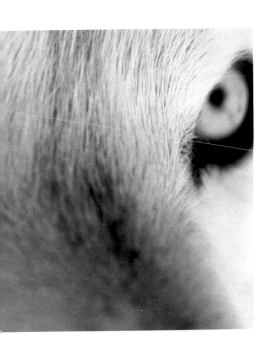

If you ain't the lead dog,

the scenery never changes.

Lewis Grizzard, Writer

If you stop
every time
a dog barks,
your road
will never end.

Saudi Arabian proverb

Women and cats will do as they please, and men and dogs should relax and get used to it.

Robert A. Heinlein, Novelist

No one appreciates the very special genius of your conversation as the dog does.

Christopher Morley, Journalist

Did you ever **walk** into a room and forget why you walked in?

I think that is how dogs **spend** their lives.

Sue Murphy

A dog can **express** more with his **tail** in seconds than his **owner** can express with his **tongue** in hours.

Unknown

80

A dog has the soul of a philosopher.

Plato, Philosopher

You can tell by the **kindness** of a dog how a **human** should be.

Don van Vliet, Musician

You can run
with the big dogs
or sit on the porch
and bark.

Unknown

A dog is the
only thing
on earth
that loves you
more than he loves
himself.

Josh Billings, Writer and humorist

A dog owns nothing,
yet is seldom
dissatisfied.

Irish proverb

I've seen a look in dogs' eyes, a quickly vanishing look of amazed contempt, and I am convinced that basically dogs think humans are nuts.

John Steinbeck, Writer

Every dog
has his day

but the nights
are reserved for the cats.

Unknown

Picture credits

pp. 4-5 © Amana Productions Inc/Getty; pp. 6-7 © Lichtsammler/Getty; pp. 8-9 © Frank Gaglione/Getty; pp. 10-11 © Ian Waldie/Getty; pp. 12-13 © Vicky Kasala/ Getty; pp.14-15 © Raimund Linke/Getty; pp.16-17 © Ryan McVay/Getty; pp.18-19 © Yoshihisa Fujita/Neovision/Getty; pp. 20-21 © Gary Randall/Getty; pp. 22-23 © Digitalcursor/Miron Kiriliv/ www.mironkiriliv.com/Getty; pp. 24-25 © GK Hart / Vikki Hart/Getty; pp. 26-27 © P J Taylor/Getty; pp. 28-29 © Robin Knight/Getty; pp. 30-31 © Philip and Karen Smith/Getty; pp. 32-33 © Tracy Morgan/Getty; pp. 34-35 © Barbara Peacock/Getty; pp. 36-37 © DAJ/Getty; pp. 38-39 ©Peter Cade/ Getty; pp. 40-41 © Jose Luis Pelaez/Getty; pp. 42-43 © Martin Harvey/Getty; pp. 44-45 © Fry Design Ltd/Getty; pp. 46-47 © Joel Sartore/Getty; pp. 48-49 © Purestock/Getty; pp. 50-51 © Roy Toft/Getty; pp. 52-53 © Roger Wright/Getty; pp. 54-55 © D-BASE/Getty; pp. 56-57 © Image Source/Getty; pp. 58-59 © Gone Wild/ Getty; pp. 60-61 © Purestock/Getty; pp. 62-63 © Valerie Shaff/Getty; pp. 64-65 © Compassionate Eye Foundation/Jetta Productions/Getty; pp. 66-67 © Angela Martini/Getty; pp. 68-69 © Ryan McVay/Getty; pp. 70-71 © Monica Dal-masso/Getty; pp. 72-73 © Kendall McMinimy/Getty; pp. 74-75 © Jessica Peterson/ Getty; pp. 76-77 © Stockbyte/Getty; pp. 78-79 © American Images Inc/Getty; pp. 80-81 © Nathalie Mullen-Briquet/Getty; pp. 82-83 © Juliet White/Getty; pp. 84-85 © IMAGEMORE Co., Ltd/Getty; pp. 86-87 © Thomas Northcut/Getty; pp. 88-89 © Ryan McVay/Getty; pp. 90-91 © scruffy dog photography/Getty; pp. 92-93 © Lecorre Productions/Getty; pp. 94-95 © DAJ/Getty.